Maurice Hamer
11th October 1925 — 5th April 2016

A Life in Poetry

Maurice Hamer

Compiled and Edited by John Hamer
On behalf of St. John's Church, Newsome

A Life in Poetry

Maurice Hamer

Paperback Edition First Published in Great Britain in 2016
by aSys Publishing

ISBN: 978-1-910757-64-2
aSys Publishing 2016

In memory and celebration of the life of Maurice Hamer
11 October 1925 – 5 April 2016

All the proceeds of this anthology will be donated to St.
John the Evangelist's Church, Newsome, Huddersfield, West
Yorkshire, in perpetuity

Contents

Maurice Hamer—An Obituary

11ᵗʰ October 1925—5ᵗʰ April 2016

In Huddersfield in the 1920s, as in many other towns and cities in the industrial north, life was very hard for the 'have-nots.' Money was extremely scarce and luxuries extremely few and far between, if not completely non-existent. Most young lads of that generation and the ones preceding, could aspire only to an education cut woefully short at the age of fourteen or less and to follow their grandfathers, fathers, uncles and elder brothers into 't'mill' along with the rest of their peers. Any ambitions of 'betterment' were strictly 'not for the likes of them.'

Life was equally hard (if not more so) for the girls, too. The best they could aspire to, was to marry young and thereafter 'work their fingers to the bone' until death, struggling to make ends meet on their husband's meagre pay, living from one payday to the next, slaving for their husbands and raising their children as best they could under the circumstances.

And so it was into this very world that Maurice and his twin sister, Mavis were born, on the 11ᵗʰ October 1925 in very humble, typically northern, working-class surroundings at 3 Bent Street, Newsome, Huddersfield, Yorkshire. Their parents Hilda (neé Starkey) and Hubert, had married two years earlier and Maurice and Mavis were the elder siblings of Winifred (Winnie) who soon completed the family, being born just over three years later, in early 1929.

Hubert was employed (as were the majority of the working men of the area in those days) at one of the woollen mills which proliferated at that time, in the town suburbs and also in the valleys to the south of Huddersfield and all the way out to Marsden and Holmfirth (Last of the Summer Wine country) in the foothills of the Pennines.

Whilst still a child, Maurice and his family 'emigrated' along the Colne Valley (about 4 miles) to the village of Milnsbridge, presumably for Hubert's work and he therefore spent the rest of his childhood, his adolescence and young adulthood there. He left Crow Lane Junior School in 1939 at the tender age of 14, never having attended any form of secondary education at all, and followed his father into the dark satanic mills of pre-war Hudders-field and district.

Unfortunately Hubert succumbed to an inoperable obstruction of the bowel in his mid-40s whilst Maurice, Mavis and Winnie were still only teenagers. He had suffered from ill health for most of his short life—as did many others of his generation—after being gassed in the trenches of Flanders during the First World War.

At the tender age of 20, Maurice was conscripted into the army for National Service, spending two years in India which was the inspiration for his poem 'A Train Journey' and which presumably was taken directly from his experiences there. He returned to England on leave for three months in 1947 and following that, upon arrival back at Liverpool docks, expecting to be shipped back to India for a further, indeterminate period, was immensely relieved to discover that he, along with the rest of his unit had been suddenly and unexpectedly 'de-mobbed.'

On 3rd July 1948, Maurice married Doreen Wilkinson, whom he had known for several years, having met her as part of the local, teenage Milnsbridge crowd, before his long sojourn to India. They spent a far from idyllic honeymoon in Morecambe, which was notable only for its lack of romance and for the pitifully shy Maurice, spending his wedding night doing a spot of all-night fishing with someone he had met only that day, rather than fulfilling his expected conjugal duties. However, 'things' must have taken their natural course in that regard eventually, otherwise I would not be here writing this piece, now.

By the time that I was born in July 1952, Maurice had become a foreman in the finishing department at one of the local woollen mills but in so doing had had to move house an almost unthinkable, eight whole miles to the tiny village of Jackson Bridge, known locally and colloquially at the time as 'Jigby,' in the heart of 'Last of the Summer Wine' country. At their departure from all their family, friends and neighbours, there were apparently, many tears shed and promises made for reciprocal visits and exhortations of not to forget their roots etc. A very different world indeed.

In 1956, with the new 'you've never had it so good,' post-war world now presenting many previously unavailable opportunities for enhancement, to anyone who had the desire and the mental wherewithal to better themselves,

Maurice finally escaped the confines of the mill yard for the first (but not the last) time in his life. He became a travelling vacuum cleaner repair-man for the Hoover Company. Despite his relief at escaping from the dreary, repetitive and soulless life of the millworker, unfortunately the salary that Hoover paid was pitiful and Doreen and Maurice struggled to feed and clothe their four-year old (ie. me) and their new baby, Paul who had now arrived on the scene in December 1956.

And so it was that he finally admitted defeat and returned to the mill once again and for the next ten years or so, Maurice reluctantly struggled on with his dreams of escaping yet again from the suffocating twilight world of the woollen industry, constantly hoping against all hope for another opportunity of some kind to present itself. This would not manifest itself until much later, but in the meantime, Maurice had developed his talents as a singer, having built a small following as a 'club' and pub singer on the local circuit. Despite this, he had always been a shy man and was very nervous of appearing on stage—even to relatively small audiences.

In fact in 1960, he had entered a nationwide talent contest, a forerunner of 'The X-Factor' if you will, and somehow found himself in the grand final at the Floral Hall in Southport. Amazingly he won the competition outright, the first prize of which was a recording contract with Decca Records. Despite many pleas from friends and family of 'not to be so stupid,' Maurice's acute shyness and nervousness of any form of limelight prevailed and he duly turned-down the one golden opportunity of his lifetime to fulfil his wish to leave the drudgery of mill life forever.

He had another 'claim to fame' in this regard too, though. His next door-but-one neighbour was the uncle of the entertainer Roy Castle, who had himself been brought-up in the Holme Valley and on several occasions Maurice would play the piano and sing (and vice versa) with Roy, albeit in private and for family entertainment only.

It was also around this time that Maurice began to read avidly. Some inherent drive within, to educate himself 'properly' maybe? Who knows? But his extensive thirst for knowledge was to finally culminate in his passion for poetry and this book is a celebration of those poetic talents, which were no doubt nurtured and fed by his passion for reading and the wisdom that brings. I also feel that as with artists of all disciplines, there is very often a desire to rid themselves of their own deep angst and pent-up emotions which often have no other outlet, especially in men of Maurice's generation and station in life. As you read the poems in this book, you may well understand exactly what I mean.

But anyway, in the late 1960s, he finally fulfilled his desires to escape the mill forever by applying for and being offered the job of 'Education Welfare Officer' as it was known in those days. This position was in fact the updated and politically corrected version of what used to be known in the bad old days as the 'School Board Man' or truant officer and whose only function was to ensure the attendance at school of his charges by any means necessary, even force and with scant regard for the underlying reasons for their non-attendance. But, by those days, things were a little more enlightened than they had been prior to that point and Maurice's task was to form a liaison between the child, the parent and the school and to address any underlying issues that may be preventing a child from attending, regardless of apportionment of blame.

By all accounts he was excellent at his job and quickly became a well-respected member of the team, becoming well-known for his old-fashioned, caring yet firm attributes and his success rate in convincing many a hitherto un-cooperative child and its parents of the 'wisdom' of regular attendance at school.

Maurice spent the remaining twenty three years of his working life as an Education Welfare Officer, a title which eventually became Education Social Worker, helping many families (both parents and children alike) through their difficulties, receiving many accolades from those families, his colleagues, superiors and the schools with whom he liaised. Indeed upon his retirement he received a particularly glowing tribute from one of the schools with which he dealt and which is contained in an addendum to these pages as an example of the esteem in which Maurice was held by all those who knew and worked with him.

By 1957, Maurice, Doreen and family had moved from Jackson Bridge via Scholes to Honley, also in the Holme Valley, where we two boys were to spend most of our childhoods, growing up amongst the meadows, streams and woodlands of that idyllic area. For twenty five years, and long after the children had 'flown the nest' Maurice and Doreen lived in the same house, finally departing in 1982 for a much smaller (and humbler) abode, a mere stone's throw away.

From there it was another short 'hop' to a small house at Castle Hill with its wonderful panoramic views over the Holme Valley and Emley Moor—and not quite so wonderful panoramic views in the other direction, across Huddersfield towards Mirfield and beyond. They left there in 1989 to another suburb of Huddersfield, Longwood, as Castle Hill was becoming less practical and manageable for them as they entered their mid-sixties, but they were soon on the move again to Highburton, then Edgerton and finally Newsome. Dad had by this time come 'full circle'—born in Newsome then returning there at the age of 71 to his birthplace, where he would live for the remaining twenty years of his long, full life.

In fact, it was on his return to his 'roots' that he began attending Church at St. John the Evangelist in Newsome. Here he remained a faithful member of the congregation and a stalwart of the church choir until shortly before he passed away. He made many good friends at St. John's, not least of whom were the ministers, David Kent, Stephen Gott, and Ian Jamieson, who was to conduct his very moving funeral service. At least one member of the Church, June Richardson, would attribute their own return to the fold to the gentle persuasion and encouragement of Maurice. He could add evangelist to the many other titles.

In the very early 2000s, Maurice was instrumental in the project to set up a charity shop to the benefit of the local community, to be situated in Newsome village itself. The 'Together Shop' has not only continued to raise money for the local Churches but has also allowed them to offer grants to community projects. Moreover, the shop has become a community in itself, where local people – churchgoing and non-churchgoing – have enjoyed the fellowship of volunteering together. It was for these sterling efforts that Maurice was nominated by the Wakefield diocese to receive the Queen's Maundy Money at Wakefield Cathedral in 2005, an honour of which he was extremely proud — and rightly so.

Maurice began writing poetry sometime in the mid to late 1970s, at first just largely incoherent scribblings which at least served their purpose as an outlet for his pent-up frustrations and emotions, gradually becoming more lucid and proficient as time slowly passed. Eventually his skills developed to a level whereby he felt comfortable entering local poetry competitions, winning several small prizes and having two or three published over time. But he was never a publicity-seeker or one to push himself forward, preferring instead to merely write for his own satisfaction and enjoyment.

Indeed, after his passing and whilst sorting through his copious papers, I was amazed to discover just how much poetry and prose he had actually written. The selections contained within these pages are merely the (more or less) complete ones. There were many, many others either partially written or too unintelligible to publish.

Poetry in fact was just one of the many hobbies he acquired over his long lifetime. In the 1950s and 1960s, he was also an accomplished Crown Green bowler, travelling all over the North of England to competitions, several of which he won. He also had developed a love for gardening whilst living in the house at Honley, with its large garden, most of which was given over to every kind of vegetable imaginable. Again, Maurice's competitive spirit came to the fore and he won prizes at local shows for his cabbages, peas and swede etc., on several occasions.

In the late 1990s, sadly Maurice's hearing began to fail him and somewhat more seriously, his vision. He was diagnosed with macular degeneration; a serious, incurable and progressive condition whereby the sufferer loses all central vision and even this central 'hole' in one's sight eventually becomes larger and larger until one is left with the smallest amount of peripheral vision only, and even that is blurred. Long before the end of his life, Maurice was registered blind even though he was still partially sighted. Of course once his sight had deteriorated beyond a certain point, then all reading, writing and even watching TV became impossible. His literary 'career' was now over.

I am sure that had he retained his sight, then this book would have been much larger and there is no doubt in my mind that his passion for poetry writing would have continued on, instead of being restricted to around a twenty-year period from the late 1970s to the late 1990s.

Then in early 2011, his wife Doreen sadly passed away after a short illness at the age of 83, which left him bereft. They had been married for almost sixty three years and although their relationship was often fractious, there is no doubt that they loved each other very deeply. For the rest of that year he suffered dreadfully from his terrible loss and the family began to wonder if the grief would take its toll on him and prove fatal, but we should have known not to underestimate his strength of character, despite his seemingly soft exterior. Amazingly, he slowly recovered and although there is no doubt that he still missed her greatly, he made a new life of sorts for himself for his final five years without her.

Despite his failed eyesight, his failing hearing and the general weakening of his health as he approached ninety years old, he still managed to catch the bus every day without fail into Huddersfield and followed his own little routine, shopping for his groceries, then to the bank and to the same café every day, where I often used to meet him for a catch-up and general chit chat over a coffee—for which he always insisted on paying. Virtually everyone he came into regular contact with on that well-worn route, bus drivers, shop assistants, bank staff and the café staff alike, came to know and love him. He had that effect on most people that he met and was what is known colloquially as 'a character,'

On the day after his 90th birthday, 12th October 2015, I had arranged to meet-up as usual and was just a little worried when he failed to show at the usual time. However, later that day I learned that he had 'over-celebrated' the previous night and had spent the morning in bed as a result, so we met the next day instead and all seemed well. He was his usual old self, still full of life despite his many hearing and vision issues. But this was the last time I was ever to see the dad I knew and loved. He had been suffering from poor balance and a few days later he slipped and fell on his way into his home (not for the first time) but this time there was to be no rapid recovery—or indeed a recovery of any kind. It turned out that he had bumped his head quite severely and that he had to be taken into Huddersfield Royal Infirmary, where I visited him shortly thereafter.

On several previous occasions, Maurice had had spells in hospital suffering from both urine and chest infections and which, as they so often do in the elderly, had resulted in confusion and bewilderment until treatment prevailed. But by the time Christmas 2015 was approaching, around seven weeks later, he was still in hospital and there was no sign of his mental capacity returning to normal and it had become obvious to all, that there was now no turning back. He no longer knew or remembered we, his sons—or his grandsons, Daniel, Ryan and Jonathan, despite occasional glimmers of recognition that served only to briefly ignite hope before cruelly snuffing it out again as he would go on to relate in vivid detail how it was his intention to visit his grandparents later that day, because he had not seen them 'for a few weeks'—or to pop out to the local pub 'for a pint.'

So it was that he was eventually admitted to Newsome Nursing Home a few days after Christmas, where he was to spend the last four months of his life, in blissful ignorance of his own sad plight, at least. But Paul and I in the space of those four short months watched him turn from a relatively robust ninety-year old into almost a living corpse as he contracted yet another severe chest infection and eventually, one week before his demise, he ceased eating altogether.

On Sunday 3rd April 2016, we knew that the end was nigh when we could elicit no response from him and on Tuesday 5th April, our final visit, we were informed that the kindest course of action would be to allow him to slip quietly away—an action we agreed to without hesitation. I kissed his forehead for what was to be the last time and stroked his cheek with my hand. I thought I maybe saw a faint smile, but with hindsight perhaps that was just wishful thinking.

At 7.20pm that evening, Maurice passed away peacefully in his sleep, but any grief that we may have felt at that moment was countered by the enormous feeling of relief that his ordeal was at last over and the realisation that he was now with his beloved wife, Doreen once again—and forever.

His was an unremarkable life in many ways. Maurice was no pioneer, no great leader of men, just a simple, ordinary man of good working-class stock and his passing went completely unnoticed by the world at large, but we, his family and friends knew that in his own quiet way, he had at least left a huge mark on our worlds and we will never forget him.

Goodbye dad. We all loved you very much. May you rest in peace until we are all reunited once again.

John Hamer

John Hamer
Holmfirth, May 2016.

The Poems of Maurice Hamer 1970s to 1990s

The poems you are about to read were written during the decades of the 1970s, 1980s and 1990s, with by far the most prolific period being the mid-1980s.

I am no expert on poetry, but far more knowledgeable folk on the subject than I, have seen fit to praise him for his work and he won accolades for several of them, notably *'Revelations,' 'A Car Journey'* and *'A Train Journey,'* which, as strange as it may sound, were the only ones of which I was even aware—until his recent passing, as these were the only ones ever previously published.

As for the rest, I shall leave it for the reader to decide their merits—or otherwise. After all 'beauty is in the eye of the beholder,' as someone once famously said, and as with many other aspects of art and literature, 'likes' and 'dislikes' are extremely subjective.

I have arranged the poems in alphabetical order of titles (for want of any more appropriate method of setting them out.) Unfortunately, many were undated and so my original attempts at chronological order were soon thwarted and therefore, abandoned. Indeed some were untitled and so in that event I have titled them as per their first line.

Unfortunately, this is not a complete anthology. There were many other partial bits and pieces of verse and several extra pages of prose which were impossible to place accurately, but what you will see herein is my best attempt at compiling, the 'Complete Poetic Works of Maurice Hamer.'

Some of these 69 poems are quite 'dark' and others amusing in their own way. Some are brief and others quite lengthy but hopefully, there will be something within these pages, for everyone. Maurice's unseen by most, private character is certainly apparent in many of them.

I do hope that this small volume brings you some pleasure—and those of you who knew him personally will no doubt gain a little more insight into his own private world and it will at very least serve as a reminder to you of who he was, and help his memory to live on.

Enjoy!

A Life in Poetry

Maurice Hamer

A Ballad of a Dejected Man

Refreshed by tempering, chastening clouds,
Of soothing mists, and freshing rain,
Beneath, a pageantry of darker hues,
Engulfed by vintage from the witches brew;
Bitter blends of blood-filled tears
Which stain and glint the unforseeing eye,
Scarred unholy, deep, by anguish sorely meted,
Shocked and spurred from broken bouts of grumbled sleep,
Reach out to banks of distant comfort,
Quicken, stir sad heart to reap;
Misted eyes still pining for repentance
Dismissing rancour from the fateful brood,
Out there avoiding guiling conflict,
Soar above the soulful wounds;
Breathless slopes of lush green pasture,
Windswept, wafting on a swathe of sighs,
Stealth of step will surely bolster
Feelings of exhausted pride;
Real and unreal quests are faded;
Retreat receded in the field of play,
Numbed, disjointed, mid strife of understanding
Faithless aims and meanings are to say
Mercy's door stays still and silent,
Feeble hands will not be moved,
Mind unsearching for a saving virtue,
Awesome ploys, the soul denudes;
Rank seeds are suckled in the soil of life,
Whose tendrils urge their sensuous ilk to light;
Look back to comforts of the purging womb
And glide unerring to the vale of life.

A Ballad of a Maudlin Man

Walk tall, midst the intrigues of the baser life,
Walk tall, with doleful eyes a-gleaming,
The searing plunges of the subtle blade,
Give spur and spark to meaning.

Withdraw from fateful conflict,
Or see yourself
Entwined in true demeaning,
Walk tall.

Breathless on a windswept precipice,
Your footfall will grow stronger,
Though torn twixt doubt and truth,
All retreats receding.

Stifled and choked by artful blows
Or faithless aims and meaning,
Relief through pardon and repent
As escaped all reason.

Doubts are sown and cast
And the cancer grows and grows
But from the comforts of the past,
Walk tall.

A Blue Jug

Too proud by half
to please the potter
and the poets art.
This blue squat cousin
of some Grecian urn,
has used its hieroglyphics
to make me think about,
hot toddy and mulled ale,
a blue dahlia in still life,
and black robed tribesmen
riding their white stallions
across an arid plain.
It is not enough for me,
I want to grab this
glazed piece of arrogance
thrown on some magic wheel,
crush it, to see the colour
of its clay, then scatter it
on the cold paved floor
of a jug mausoleum.

A Car Journey

We drop to the warm plains of Calgary.
The razzamatazz and dust of rodeos.
Settles on the hoof-stirred sand of wood stockades,
Where cowboy dudes in Stetsons
Change from leather duds to pin-stripes,
Swap their broncos for shiny Chevrolets;
Here in a land of wheat and mineral, the Big Sky,
Protein forced from winter-frosted soil, swaying
Indecisive, to the man who tests the golden corn.
Now by Oldsmobile through Rocky Mountain lowlands,
Nine hundred miles in air-conditioned ease,
Jet-lagged in sleep to Pacific leaping salmon,
Waking in the lap of craggy peaks, giants;
Staggered at their awesome crags, eternal snow,
Erupted spine of Continents; a magic wilderness
Inhabited by ghosts of forty-niners, unstruck gold;
Where Kaska and Bella Coola Indians, loved and bred,
Trappers from the Hudson Bay, half-breeds, engineers,
who built a railway wonder of the world;
Canadian Pacific, observation cars, power for three thousand miles,
A snaking track, which binds the base of glaciers
In metal cords; pine trees by the million
Yanked from hilltops, leaving ring-worm scars;
Shot down flumes to float in vast armadas
For circus lumberjacks to roll them to devouring jaws;
Warm springs in beautiful BC;
The western towns of Hope and Salmon Arm
Shimmering in the sweat of tropic heat;
Few miles left to end a journey,
Across the bay of a thousand isles,
Where killer whales and Sock-Eye shelter,
In the north Pacific deep.

A Dream of Fair Play

This dream was of a black man,
sat in corrugated hell,
a grove of Yucca and Papyrus
on the edge of Shanty Town.
He was at a weathered table
on a bamboo chair which sagged,
penning scripts and letters
for local tribesmen.
A letter to a friend in jail;
the matter of a grievance;
tracts for politicians, in
a vivid village parlance.
For victims of injustice,
he wrote of spirit, substance,
sometimes force as well, and
the gaps between his words,
filled with blood of mother tongues.
He flowed with new ideas, so
powerful they etched themselves
into the hardwood table, and
in beads of sweat his hopes and dreams
dropped on warm red sand,
to burst like thunderbolts
from some divine magician.

A Gathering of the Matriarchs of Dreams

I know an olive forest glade
Where friends of love will meet
To tell me of their sensuous thoughts
And how to make them real.
There's more than empty, false charades
Or fantasies and dreams,
There's warmth which fills the heady days
And passion no one sees.
Still silence in a flush of sighs
Away from constant clamour,
Sweet creatures gathered in the light
To be, when spirits flower,
What are your needs, and your desires?
Fulfilment calms the raging fires.

A Nautical Tale

John, you remember the painting of us,
We were sat on a beach,
With old Jack in a bleached twill shirt
Leaning against a barnacled break-water,
Its wooden beams scoured to sponge by drifting sand,
Can't you see his strong wind-burned arm, a finger
Pointing to the horizon, the lip of the world
Caught in a grip of air and water,
Telling us stories of tall ships, the Brigs,
Barquentines, and fighting in a man o' war,
Or deck hands on a dirty British Coaster.

Our eyes would close, lost in images,
Caught in a dazzle of shell and shot, ricocheting
Through the pall of smouldering tar and timbers,
Scorched hemp, and burning oakum wedged in boards;
In that cove we sensed the yarns of smugglers
And could almost taste the barrelled rum, and feel
The nap of wild sick, and pewter jars of myrrh,
How could they circumnavigate the earth when Jack
Has said the earth is flat? A "Flat Earther,"
That if you sail a ship too far
You will slip off the edge of the world.

A Night Out at a Small Town 'Tiffany's'

I went by special invitation,
to a down-town winter party,
when spotlights in the shopfronts (of Le Bonnet and La Mode),
flick out in night arcades.
The shopping malls were empty,
no longer could they feel,
the footsteps of the window shoppers,
on gilt and frosted glass parades.
A darkened club, an upper bracket den,
a tinsel palace, small town Tiffany's;
where the young at heart takeover,
to flirt, and drink the coloured wine.

I chose the quietest corner, unseen
hot sweats across my face,
watching busty barmaids, pull
pints of lager with a smiled panache;
these for upwardly mobile,
braceletted, chain-slung men,
met to talk about their conquests
of Del Sol and Costa Brava,
the merits of real ale as well.
Smugly they lift their tankards,
Eyes intent on daring cleavages around,
and with every swing of brass-railed doors,
clouds of smoke and beery air
flushes onto winter pavements.

Outside, ledges run with condensation,
drips and grime from starling's wings,
carried in at dusk from misty country,
now preened with heat from deep fat fryers,
and boiler pipes coiled around the stores.
The Crypt is closed, for lack of funds,
and outcasts warm their fleshless bones
with chemicals and penny poisons,
drunk without a thought of harm.
Still, I want to be out there,
there on the night streets, to look at
lamps lit on posts, straight hems,
of unseen kerbs and lonely cul-de-sacs,
some which curve away past dim suburbs,
some to peter-out on the edge of a moor.

A Rural Tale

This bounteous vale of trees and dreams
On trellised sedge green sheets,
Embroidered squares on mantled hill and dales;
Majestic peaks arise, to where the wispish cotton wool of cloud,
Relaxes in impish vein;
Florid gentle rain,
Fledgling, flippish, flopping,
Cascading freshening moisture
On each pasture and its cloister,
Seducing nature's bounty from the ground;
Luscious harvest passions, meticulously fashioned,
Ripening germs of seed and fruit and flower;
Accepting summer's tenure,
Sustaining love and sinew,
Delighting rural granaries of grain.

A System

The selfish juggernaut rolls on
Relentlessly
Its flailing chains thresh
Endlessly
In the wake, bleeding flesh is left
To salve its wounds
Tracks of steel forge furrows
Through red clay
And bathe the uninformed in powdered blood
As silent victims are reforming

A Train Journey

The ornate façade of Bombay station
In the year of nineteen forty-five,
Thronged with sweaty bodies in blotchy whites and purples,
With assortments of khakis and the mottled jungle greens
Of military visitors from a distant world at war.

I sit on a latticed wooden bench in the corner,
Oppressed by the heat and lonely
In the company of mysterious languages,
Assaulted by a mêlée of world-weary travellers
And unfamiliar smells, superheated steam and oil
Propelling an iron-bellied relic of the British Raj
On a four-day journey across the miraged plains
Of India; a land of piquant spices, poverty and princes,

Between the shrouds of white cloth
My companions smile and nod approvingly
At my presence, strangely respecting an intrusion
Into their world of mysticism, dhotis and chapattis

Opposite, a holy man sits with legs crossed
Swaying to the rhythm of the train
An unbalanced, starched linen statue,
His rimless glasses and balding head
Glisten with droplets of sweat as he arrows his prayers
To heaven, like a disciple of the Mahatma.

Meanwhile the train lumbers on into the past,
Through villages of mud and cow-dung wattle,
And fluid fields of paddy, where women carry
Pitchers of water on ram-rod heads,

A colony of grey baboon nimbly lopes through scraggy
Brush of sharp scree and tufted grasses,
Whilst dhobi wallahs batter their washing
Against the bleached stones of a river,

White minarets of mosques and temples,
Standing fingers of icing-sugar cakes,
Point lazily to the vivid, azure sky,
As a betel nut-chewing passenger yawns,
Red-mouthed like a sub-continental vampire.

Three and a half sunsets now expended,
The train is weary of its load,
Eyes, nose and ears have lost the urge
To function, as we finally run out of steam
At a terminus of wonder,
Agra and the Taj Mahal

A Truth

Designs of dreams, with wounds despairing,
Reach out to fragile frames of life,
To self and kin and love, past caring,
Ruffled pride of all alike.

Poorly fashioned things performing,
Hardened pulses hold themselves at bay,
Plain feats of rest responding to each slumber
Quicken, urge sharp thoughts to say.

Break your camp in this drear region,
Pitch it on the plain of truth,
To where fresh things of minds and sweet surprises,
Await upon the wisest sooth.

A Winter Party

A winters evening in suburbia
in a mortgaged, architectured box.
Tipsy, she slips with a tray, loaded,
cocktails cascade into alcoholic showers,
liquid colour turns a shabby tight leather
skirt to wet-look, rounded thighs,
like a chameleon in the change.

... Diving glasses thud to the
parquet floor, sending green olives,
lemon slices and slivers of broken glass
scudding into dusty crevices.
Barely sober she winks and cocks
a painted thumb behind her, mouthing,
someone's making it with your wife,
there is nodded acquiescence.

It is time for summer magic,
Hammer House of Horror, in Super Kodak,
not the slides again, knobbly knees
and handkerchief squares, knotted,
or do we have to bear the nudist ones of
virile Georgie in a Rambo poseur game.

And Then What?

Then came
Ignorance and truth,
Lettered tools of shape and form
In alphabets of pictures,
The great and simple kind,
Assorted.

Seats of Bachelor's Degrees,
Academic bourgeoisie,
Met to discuss
The "chicken and the egg."
Their limitless research
Was measured out
In unfair doses.

Au Revoir Thornhill High

This is not what I asked for;
A meeting, then a time
To say goodbye, to say thanks
That I was given chance to make,
Not just a friendship
But a way of life;
I hope that you and I
Helped to push some shadows
Further from a little town.

NB. This was Maurice's parting shot to the headteacher at Thornhill High School in Dewsbury upon his retirement. It was an institution that had become a massive part of his life as an Education Social Worker and his sorrow at saying goodbye is evident in the above. Please see the addendum for the reply.

Ballad of Hope through Sound

Ballads of dreams and schemes,
Drumming on the tympani of reason,
Cacophonies of broken themes
Transposing jangled feelings.

Symphonies composed in different keys,
Melodies of sharp and flat exploding,
Sinfonia of love and hate, and new ideas,
Rhythmic phrases goading.

Baton winnowing out the raucous note,
Erupting into deep imprinted songs
Of woes and joys and hope,
Engulfing rights and wrongs.

Flute of surging, moving voice,
Spell out your comforting device
Which isolates the chances choice
Providing comforts which suffice.

Refrain from movements Allegretto,
The soothing pace of humble Largo
Fills the space of ruffled passion
On the waves of true vibrato.

Final chords of harp and drum,
Too soon their magic ceased to be,
Lulling, salving senses too become
Engulfed in near infinity.

Store this magic in the sense of tune
In safe archives from hate immune,
Return when flagging spirts wane
Restoring hope, almost in vain.

Bewitched

The body stirs,
Unable to halt the pull of a witching hour,
My silhouette detaches
An ectoplasm figure, possessed,
It melts into
The sooty stone breast of a hot fire-back,
I shout 'stop!'
But the earless phantom, a demented shape,
Scuttles west,
Over fields, through dormant bramble hedges;
It has gone
But it will return with the potions of a she-witch,
And I shall be recharged.

Bread

A feel of brown-glazed earthenware,
The powder of the corn
Warm fronds which slip through hands to share
A soft and folding form.

A dust like talcum on smooth wood,
Cool finger tips which glide
Along the alabaster mounds
Which coaxes them to life.

The earthy smell of heady wine,
A mix of oil that soothes,
The swish of silk across firm thighs,
Fresh milk and frothy brews.

The claw and squeeze of moulding flesh,
As bodies well and breathe,
Still moist and limp they cling to test
The thrill their shapes will meet.

And now a rest which comes from need,
The slow and shifting rounds
Are left to simmer in the heat
And there is not a sound.

Come to me with heart sore aching...

Come to me with heart sore aching
Rest your weary mind in mine,
Trust in faith to do the seeking,
Comforts of a kind divine.

Words so futile and beguiling
Offered up as sour wine,
Sweeten sylph your true sensations,
Give yourself in close entwine

The bands disclose their simple story,
Power and stealth be not abused
Release in time and pour your mercy,
On that sad soul so oft bemused.

Temptation slow fulfils the answer,
Accept and trust this mortal claim.
To search your problem any deeper,
Prolongs the agony of pain.

Posing them their vexing question,
Don't dismiss their gift so sane,
Melt into a fitful slumber,
Receiving love so rich, and vain.

Company

Waiting in comfortable silence,
Through a well-window a leaden sun
Toys with dust on a casement,
And a warm west wind teases out
Sentiments from a plaited curtain pull,
Moving it in eccentric circles,
A hurdy-gurdy, a dumb metronome
Or a curled finger which says, 'come!'

The morning paper lies crumpled, out of reach,
And slippered heels slide forward in unison
Creasing the soft pile of a mohair rug;
I am expectant and warm, indulgent
Of sounds which test my patience,
A boy whose footsteps are too loud,
And the bark of a neurotic dog.

Shall I be lost for words, words left unsaid,
Unsold apologies, unposted thoughts, a smile
Not returned, but left in an aberration;
The skid of cars making an entrance,
Accelerating away, with other noises
Lost in disappointment, but now

A pause, the dusk, a presence,
The muffled knock of a gloved hand,
The squeak of a dry hinge, a latch lifting,
The scene, the aura, the voice
And at last the touch which said all.

Confessions of a Fir Tree

I did not ask to leave
The patch of rotted mulch
Where I was bred, a sapling
Safe among the cones and branches
Touching other long lean frames;
Until a woodman's lethal cut
Sent the sap to bleed from me,
Drop by drop, pushed into a life,
A centre piece for winter parties.
Drop by precious drop, no longer
Could I bear the weight of snow,
Tinder dry and bare, a tinsel star
Atop my point of stunted growth
Had faded in a winter wind
Because it envied Bethlehems.
Choirs with lanterns sang around
Me one cold eve, they must have
Found the will to praise a Saviour,
But now the crackers linking friends,
The shrivelled carcass of a turkey,
Left to blow around an empty square.
Peace on earth, goodwill as well.

Don't relax your vigil

Don't relax your vigil for the truth,
Means so sensible and kind,
Search for answers from the sooth,
Entrusted with the life refined.

Bubbled passion spilling out its wrongs
Hopes for comfort in the sky,
Wisdom slowly seeping through the throng
To meet the will of those who chose to try.

Bend your knee and ask for help,
In self-fulfilment of your higher needs,
Let those darts of humble asking, quench
The burning spirit searching for the seed.

Draw in those thundering vibrations,
Salve of righteousness itself,
Quelling turgid feelings of impatience
Rewarding feelings with great wealth.

Bow in humbling obedience,
Answers will pour out to you,
Loaded with the help of reverence,
Support and succour for a life anew.

Don't you know?

Don't you know how to love?
Don't you know what it means?
Don't you know from the saints above
that <u>love</u>,
is what it means?

Emotional Rationality

The eyes of a man frustrated,
The eyes of a man in pain,
The eyes of a man worn down by care,
The eyes of a doting man.

But where is the man who really cares,
Where is the man who will,
Where and how does he start to see
The progress he's making toward hell?

Man of guilt, man of shame,
Man with the mote in his eye,
He lifts himself up to smash himself down
And does it again and again.

Coming from the kernel of the man
Is a vibrant warmth,
In an icy pause,
Is a feeling of yes I can,
But is he real,
Does he feel?

The link between man and man is
A flirtation,
A disease,
A disaster,
Because the third of the triad requires – love.
An experience,
Justice
And a quelling of frustration to achieve.

Where is the man who can understand?
Where is the man who perceives?
Keep out of my life all suckling types
And give yourself to the damned,
To his bosom he will receive.

Use not on me the guile of youth,
Nor sickening shameful ploys,
Though I ask for care
And produce it not,
My need is just as real.

The mind flies in circles,
Ducking, and
Wheeling,
Accepting,
Avoiding,
Imprisoned by a selfish need;
Where is he who understands?

Offer me not the diluted sops
Got from a barren soil,
My inward heart needs strength
And joy
And warmth;
Is what I am seeking an impossible dream
To expect and not receive?
Or am I to wilt in the searching?

My horizons do not narrow,
My need is for outstretched hands,
To conjure the perfect joining
Of friendship made as one.

Drive me not to the narrow way
Which stifles bores and decays,
Show me a man who understands
And I'll show you a man in pain.
The drive of youth,
The spirit of youth,
Will flourish
But will soon decay;
What will replace them?
A charitable heart,
Or a lust and a greed.

Who am I to expose myself?
To imprison my caring heart?
I loved so well,
I fought so well
But I relinquished my right to succeed.

Evolutionists Diary circa 2000

Someone once said, all this
began with a BANG!,
when frog's legs, the skin of sea lizards,
manicured toe nails of a Yeti,
cods heads and the underbelly of snakes,
appeared in the bowel of an ocean.

From them came man,
evolved I say, by natural selection.
So here I am, by a shore, watching fish
in a warm salt wash of smooth pebbles;
but I have news for them,
their chance of survival is slim.

Have you heard about the hole,
the one in the ozone layer?
Caused by chemicals from aerosols;
its as big as a continent
and lets in ultra violet from the sun,
does something unpleasant to life.

And did a rib from Adam
make the first feminist
or the first nuclear disarmer;
and who started the trend
in pornographic telegrams
between estranged lovers in the 60s.
BANG!

And did you hear the news?
because of atomic attack,
Prime Ministers Question Time
is postponed until tomorrow,
post-nuclear weather permitting;
in the meantime there will be
an interlude of music composed jointly
by the Angle-Soviet music appreciation society;
with special effects created by the sound
of nuclear missiles in the upper atmosphere,
travelling at phenomenal speeds; rather like
Concorde on a summer Sunday flight.
BANG! Bang. Bang.

I Wonder

Now the ground is hard with hoar frost,
The cathedral spire crusted with snow,
Where are the tanned bodies which rummaged
Through branches on trunks of lemon trees,
Groping for ripe shapes, slung heavy
In shaded alleys of the groves?
And blades of grass bruised by sandals,
A patch of sand that bore our rumps
In salty warmth on a stretch of shore.
If we could return will there be new growth,
And if wind and tide have spared
These minute summer islands,
Will the same grains once more
Wrap themselves around our willing form?

In the Shadow of too Many Sighs

In the shadow of too many sighs,
Those loves of life give up and dance to me
Their incandescent glory of delight
That none shall better see;
Except in portraits of a life, which has
Which holds in majesty of vanity
Black and gold, in colours patently
Convey the travesty of things, that we
So well informed of honesty
Give so little modesty of love;
Silver and silence in the dawn of fresh desire,
Now recedes the answer of a subtle hour,
With gentle creatures stood in sweet retire,
Time unspent the faces of the bower
Entreat the song of new unsinging joy;
Not now the feel of ruptured power
Nor the rush of self's incessant clamour
For an antiseptic balm
To savour in a second pallor.

Indecision

Reasoning, wavering,
Satisfying, quavering
Indulge yourself you fool.
Enjoy yourself in torrid tasks,
Go on, break the rule

You'll win each one
If guile you use
And cut off all retreat,
Indulge yourself, demean yourself,
Go on, break the rule.

Is True Humility the Sign?

Does the sorrow of our travel
Come to ought, in mindful sight
Of hungered souls ensnared in mammon's fearful hold,
Acting out the humour and the love of faded light.

Do the cast play out their part
In quiet conscience of a humble spark?
Which each turn of dice, turns from head to heart
And back again to sample life's false art.

Self-desire, embroidered gracefully with craft;
Outward casts its line of barbed nets
To innocence of truth with joy and laughter
Not aware of jabbered soulless sets.

Oh, innocence of love, not I,
Not yet the comforts of the humble hour,
Nor the peace transcribed on cloudless sky,
Until in me resolves the restless bower.

June 12th 1987

On our estate the war with bottles never stops,
But there is a glass recycling plant,
Worn tyres on untaxed cars crush it, till the streets
Look like the stained glass of churches,
And when the sun decides to shine, they look as if
They're paved with diamonds.

Last week's wash hangs limp on knotted cords,
Draped down wild privet hedges,
Youths with short cropped hair, T-shirt Union Jacks,
Think they're National Front supporters
And dabble in the latest cults, consulting
Ouija boards in garden huts.

Rotted window frames, brown stains on gable ends,
Rubbish left to rot,
Damp which creeps down paths and under doors
To meet with condensating walls,
When the rent man calls, it's always spent,
And if the credit drapers
Dodge the packs of angry mongrel dogs,
They sell their shoddy on the 'never-never.'

Virtue hurried past our cul-de-sac,
Perhaps it couldn't stop
When the kids were bad with whooping cough,
I suppose we're lucky
On a windless day we can hear an evening bell,
And talk of investments.

But we have *our* shares in squalor.

Library

Collection of words, mixtures of people
In fact and fiction
Drawn to odours of ink and new paper.

A gorgeous assistant
Who smells of romance, and luxury soap,
A starched dress of print.

Her lovely black bow on titian hair
To the nape of her blouse,
Don't stare too long or she's likely to blush.

Through fashion glasses
She'll show you the isms and ologys
In stunted silence.

Disharmony on the history rack,
Marx and Disraeli
Debating for the best place in the stack.

Fun in the fiction,
Heathcliffe and Cathy are having a love-in
On page sixty seven.

Oliver Twist is reading "The Gourmet,"
On top of all that
Fagin's been caught with his hand in a wallet.

Oozing lime, lollies
Stuck all over my best fashion trousers,
Mothers there browsing.

Original thoughts, and philosophy
Never said before
Is more than likely to be a fallacy.

Lovers

It is too late now
Since the last brush of hands
Excited,
And a muffled snigger on the line
Shut out
The tight spring of minds,
Which led
To the burial of two lovers,
One here
The other who knows where,
Though parted
Were from habit stuck fast,
Knowing
How to climb into each other's thoughts,
Victims
Of the extra sensory.

Maggie

Ginger and pepper, barley and herbs,
All mixed up in a bundle of verve,
Green and brown and spotted too,
Managed by Maggie from Kalamazoo.

Bodies of spice in bubbling bowls,
Bottles fermenting in secretive holes,
Relish and rice of savoury pique,
Maggie's a master of aromatics.

Marginals

They call you marginals
Shadows in a city,
There must have been a choice
Your God is still our God,
Trapped in a cloister
Without a crucifix,
Your graft is deviant,
Has no market value,
You will pay penalties
For not flying a balloon
Across a summer ocean,
Or walking to the Pole
Alone, single handed;
People in the afterglow
Claw, bleeding finger-tips
Build yourself a stage.

Marionette

like it or not
when the bell rings
you will perform
a body trapped
in coils of wire
your spinal chord
will click out of joint
nerve ends will split
four ways at once
you will not know
your left from your right
a compass needle
behind your head
will fix toward
magnetic north
leaving you slung
at the mercy of
the puppeteer.

Maude Says

Our Miss Humble, Maude we call her, says,
Things haven't been the same, lets see… since 1979.
The village children's dreams are lost, their portions gone,
Trim homes of flint, a snip, they can't afford,
And the Shire horse at Hundred Acre Farm, shakes its head
At Ford Granada Ghias; the Vicar's Morris Minor
Looks ashamed to share the road with them, people,
Head-banded, hell bent on fitness, the instinct to survive.

Boxwood and Beech do not whisper to the thatch,
Washed stone weathers with the smooth grip of a plough
And young shoulders may never feel the rip of blades
Through fallow soil, still hungry for its pride.
Maude was really cross, when they changed the corner shop,
They don't sell groceries now, only antique bric-a-brac.

South winds still brush across the stacks,
But the smoke of the past, hangs in coils of sadness.
Now the young have gone to earn their merit marks
In platoons of unemployed there they must prove
Their "fitness to survive."
Will they never visit Maude again?
For apple falls and oven bottom pies.

Men at Castle Point

That uncertain day,
where Castle Point
juts in white water,
a priory basks
in moss and lichen
clung to salted rock.
The current destined
to join a tide,
with the hurry
of a winter wind.

I knew those men
at the end of the sea;
one tossed pebbles,
the other slow
to round the headland.
They seemed oblivious
before the surge
a warning of the bore,
splitting and sinking
islands of sand,
to cut off the shore.

Helpless, crippled,
I remembered them
once as swimmers,
but they were old now,
the reaping waves
beyond them.
Numb with fear,
ill at case, alone,
I called for help
from the priory's
prayer filled stone.

Mentor

His inner-ears were shot, degenerated
stirrup bones, bells and waterfalls oscillating
through a tinnitus-addled skull, but his
inner-self wanted to walk, and walk,
across the North York moors and Southern Downs,
to the East preferably, always to the East.

I have sat in the company of this special friend,
in comfortable silence, sincerity, he valued that,
selfless he denounced the 'I' as selfishness,
loved theology, and Cappie his pitman's dog
as black as a Geordie coal-face, once he
dared to love again, and kicked the altar in disgust.

NB. This was a tribute to Maurice's lifelong best friend and mentor, the late John Heads who before his retirement had been vicar of Paddock, Huddersfield for many years.

Money Spinners

in this vision
thoughts are not always
delicate in form

many patterns
from days long gone
memory faded

insistence that we must
remember the dead of wars
lest we forget

red flowers to remind us

what of the words
plaited by silver tongues
which do not say

my daddy was a slave
and the feet and hands
of his child bled

chasing a legless mule
on splintered floors
before the day began
to the end of night

twisted and turned
stretched and curled
for a pittance

spun for harshest winters
and the sweat of summers
toil trapped in the fibre of shrouds

fashions for luckless children
designed to satisfy
the masters of mammon
lest we forget

there were corpses to remind us.

Moonlight

Anything above the height of chimneys
Is difficult to understand, except
The brightness of the moon, hung
On yellow autumn sky, an aspic model
In translucent clay, to alert the dusk
Of some unearthly glow, that will
Burst upon the dark, and open up
A corner of some forgotten field,
Or illuminate the still dank alleys.
Pick out the treasure in a stack of rubble
Moonlit green and purple in a breakers yard,
And in a phosphorescent glare, see
The shadow of a feathered clawking clown
Swoop across the warm curled imprint
Of a vixen's resting place on flattened down.
I would like to lift my arms to praise
Astronomers, or technicians of the light,
Pushed by clouds and bounced from stars
To catch a line of ants along the flattened dirt;
And in candle-rush hear a cock crowing,
And wait until the next agenda of the night.

Mute

Do not swallow or draw breath
Until the last shadows
Fall deathly quiet
On a cloth of still water.
Do not sleep fast
For fear the disgruntled
Rumbling of a nightmare
Sheds into a balmy dawn.
Oil the cogs in the clock of your head
In the fat from the milk of silence.
Walk naked
So that a starched bodice
Does not crackle against the body,
Or a feather drop
To the nap of a lamb's wool rug.
Walk with me
To where a warm west wind
Accentuates
Our feel and touch in the hushed rhythms
Of a bolero on a beach of down.
In strands of grass
Dormant after a summer surge,
Watch the far north
Drip with blue, pink and reds
Left from a redundant Borealis.
With the poise of a puppet
And the costume of a harlequin
Choose the mimicry of a clown.

Ode to a Social Worker

How can you judge
That you do know
Each wills exact delight?

How can you hope
To meet the need
Of their perplexing plight?

Do you accept
Their inner man;
Presume to feed their minds?

How can you plan
The path they chose
And turn it into light?

How can you give
These better things
With offerings so trite?

Accept yourself
For what you are…
A vain, innocuous mite.

Oh! How I long to understand

Oh! How I long to understand,
This thing, this place in life,
Oh! How I need it deeper now
Than all the saints in strife;
I need your wounds to set me free,
I need your humble life,
Dear Lord, Sweet God,
Please humble me,
And lead me to the light.

Original Thought

How many are drawn,
to collections of words,
the smell of ink
and new paper?

Only to find
it's all been said
before.

Peas

In an alley near a dye-polluted stream
Playing "truth or dare" and "tag,"
Underneath a gas lamp, with a gang
Wishing I could reach its iron arm,
And when I was a swank with the Scouts
A show-off to the Brownies in a wood,
Or listening to the 78s of Harry James
Someone should have had the wit to say!

When my seaside outing train
Broke down in a two mile tunnel,
With 300 smoke-soiled Oddfellows
They should have said!
Or doing clubs, with ballads of Sinatra
And anthem solos in the Chapel choir,
Petting with precocious misses, at a hop,
Someone should have whispered in my ear

About 'The Sound'
Pulsed the nerve endings,
Ripples from base drum to snare,
Like sand rushing through a fine cane screen,
When it stopped – it left a vision
Of the Caribbean, shanties on a beach
Spotted headsquares,
It was, aesthetically of course
Dried peas rattling in a tin.

Prisoner

Looks easy, all I have to do
Is step outside the door,
Down a patio with a view
Across an open moor.

However, I have hit some snags,
Not least the dry stone walls,
And fresh cut fields of meadow grass
Near woods of sycamores.

I could walk toward the sky-line
From hill top to hill top,
Traverse a gorge with scented pines
And down a granite rock.

Damned woods and fields, encircling walls
Why won't you set me free?
You'd much prefer to have my soul
Incarcerated here.

Rain

A bough cushions the fall
drops slither groundwards
on veins and stems
to criss-cross wrinkles on craggy bark
gathering at the base
stagnant in an earthy mould

They dam and sink
to rise as springs ice cold
leaf pontoons ferry to fledgling streams
which worm around stumps
down sodden banks
polishing coarse grass and laying it flat

Whirlpools turn in small ponds
and fizzle out expended
as skirts of brown tide
lap against the shallow edges
drawing in dead vegetation
to a scum which dissipates

Growth is inevitable
roots and soil are quenched
sources merge in tides of breakers
to plummet over granite
in a bubbling cataract
levelling in the deep swell

There is overspill into stone gulleys
to wooded valleys
enticing litter
to join the pot-pourri of stew
in spacious rock pools
to catch their breath in eddies
surge across boulders
making white water.

Redirected Vanity

Reams of light, legions pulses in the after-glow,
Going there to snatch the crumbs of pain to bear
On restless days and nights of vivid contrasts
Sucking in last sops of vain subduing might,
Disgorged on tips of heath and fen,
Nulling crimes of contest, washing tides of stealth,
Fluid senses swinging side to side
And driving on to match the magnet's cloying hold;
Who are you souls of flesh and blood alone?
You people of the after-low,
Your pretence is of the baser kind
Unaware of persons of the strife;
Thro' succession of the shallow things
Succeed you mundane beings,
Succeed and die, dissolve;
Remember this you vainer types of life and love
Exhausting battles fought and won
In temperatures which start and startle,
All rewards of conflicts lost;
You vain, drear, wanton creatures of the after-glow,
Pretend you are the sons of life,
Go on pretend in complex comforts;
This plane provides no solace for the hosts of them
Who pine for comforts given, abused,
And followed by demise;
Death of itself should be a milestone,
Reward of conflicts lost,
Research in greater glory
Of what was won and past;
Depend on academic stealth, depend
On structures lived, imposed, contrived,
Your end is so decisive and despised;
You must try, yet still you'll die
Protecting vanity and stealth,

You insipid things, go to gather harvests of the after-glow,
This glow was fashioned by a thousand eyes
Of bliss and love so sore abused,
Blessed by principles
Designed by them
Who glory in and gorge themselves in Death.

Revelations

Stretch out in the stubble of corn
And let straw cling to washed denim,
With your chin cupped in caring hands
Look toward the split level habitat
Framed under the belly of a milk cow,
It is dancing in a haze, precarious on a spur
With garden walls bedded in flaking rock
Unsure foundations, and a trellis of vapour trails
Which distort the symmetry of a doomed artefact.

A trimmed poodle paws after Emperor butterflies,
But its pomaded fists are slow
In the cloud of incinerated compost,
Above, the map of a new world
In pleasing clerical grey, silhouetted
Against blossom pink to orange,
And edged in supernatural crimsons.

Must we wait for a golden arm to reach down
To massage and comfort the nervous systems
Of the ambitious, stressed professionals and factions,
Cliques, parties, mercenaries and uneasy militia,
The powerful and powerless.
Sieve and refine, pour out the dross
And bury this land clinging to its poisons,
Plait silken ladders, mould a coral escalator,
And climb.

Self Esteem

Here is a need which should accede to true delights,
And is necessity for inward dreams
Reviving love and life;
Without this prop of so-called self,
Would decay the inner calm,
Used in proper form
Directing, searching for the art of love
Which stimulates the contrite man;
Do not decry this greed for self's true needs,
To offer, take each man's rewards
And turn them into things of flesh and blood,
From which will come delights;
Not in abstract naked forms,
But fullness fit to offer to the light,
Experiences which glow with right,
Right through self, assuaged by truth,
That man's abilities survive
If so refined, by might of self-fulfilment;
Don't deny the things so tried
Offer it through self denied
And with confidence of will,
Dulling all those erring, doubting minds,
Which decry humility the sign,
True self perpetuates the kindling will of man,
Forging fortunes fit and kind.

Shoes

Soft with the green juice of lawns
Paper thin soles to feel a farthing underfoot.
On frosty nights they have stood,
Felt the breath of stones,
Seen the pincered patterns,
Carried me through hillside ginnels, warrens
Of weavers cottages, where boughs
Click on roofs of weathered slate,
And in gas light, behind the chintz, seen
Bobbed heads, labouring.
We have walked in catacombs
Of mills, vertical, cellared, without day,
Or along dam banks, where gulls are free.
Made to walk on grass,
Willed on the kiss of a bowl on jack,
Taken their wearer to task, in a tiff with a lover.
No hurry like winged heels,
They plod with time to see injustices,
And hear the tongues of prejudice.
I shall care for them, because they have
A gift of bearable pain.

Sleeping Partners

That evening how I longed to speak,
To say how much I cared,
As the gaps between our slippered heels
Were moving ever wider.

Your face had thoughts of someone else,
You poured one drink,
My mind was blank and so intense
I could not mention him.

You were already asleep when I put out the light,
But I saw where a tear
Had trickled from the corner of a mascara'd eye
Staining the white sheet.

There was a stillness, I could smell the dark,
I wanted to hold you,
To smooth your hair along the cover
Soothe your longings.

I could not help the scenes, the past events,
Our uncertain feelings,
Was it my insecurity or thoughtlessness?
Perhaps our incompatibility.

Slim Truths

Slim truths to pickle head and heart,
With wandering strands of pulses frayed,
By the frenzied beat and mists which start
To crumble in the fearless day.

Compulsive mind agog, adrift to baffle
Souls in quest, for answers trusted in the sway
Of languid words and garbled syllables,
Endowed with whispering spirits of the deity.

In this void of fractured day
Are the charms, the harms of life,
This plan so rife with revelations of a kind
Which stir and humble simple vanity.

Soliloquy

For you, white flowers,
Black ribbon for your hair,
To care is not in fashion, but
You brought it
Angel rare,
To soothe a trouble,
Still unknown.

From you, comes music
Of a gentle mind,
With loving thoughts,
Which you dear,
Give so freely,
With a precious smile.

From you, a voice
Which drifts across
The space of time,
To lift a sadness
Angel rare,
In this wait of silence,
Tinged with near despair.

Your poise and bearing,
Dressed in tasteful fashion,
Brogues and denim
You possess,
Chiffon, tweed, to satisfy
A lovely woman's fancy.

If we ever meet,
Shall I be lost for words,
Words left unsaid,
Apologies, unposted thoughts,
Angel rare,
Do I cry into shadows
Of an aberration?

I sit in expectation,
And watch a leaden sun
Toy with dust on windows,
While warm west winds
Tease out sentiments,
From a silken curtain pull.

I fantasise a visit,
A pause in the dusk,
Your voice, your aura,
Your presence
Angel rare,
And at last a touch
Which melts the soul.

Still Life

Locked in time, the trials of the humble and the vain,
Stored to harvest when dew is on the mould,
Mysteries imprinted on the matter of the mind,
Interpreted by skilful, foolish souls;
Who put wisdom in the ground of life,
Where intellect will vanish just the same?
Love is wasted in a land of fools,
Where is that which heals all pain.

Ten Finger Exercise

Hung on – finger-tip hung on
Temper
Puffy eyes
Conscience
Almanacs of words and form
The Telegraph
Page Three in the Sun
Final rate demand
Poetry
Dare you listen to the distance?
Accept kind hearts without coronets?
Say you care
Vote S.D.P
Worship in a church
Live in a canary yellow coach
With heavy rock and socialism
I almost got there – but came back,
Like climbing a rock-face upside down.

That Day

I am reminded of that day,
when a better part of me
thought that all my sins
were once for all completed.

Your surprising invitation for
a lunch-time drink, with hope
that you could point our thoughts
from stilted, guilty conversation,
to other things we had to say.

If you spoke I did not hear,
only strangled thoughts
to keep the body yearning,
and all our friendly gestures,
lay unfinished in the air.

That day, I am inclined to think,
we were wrapped in shrouds,
which surely must have made
a hurtful vow of silence.

The Affair

Life was very good,
The woman with a sad, plain face,
Her form beneath a dowdy dress
Looked rare, her body language was uncanny;
In the hubbub of an office
Her perfume choked the senses,
A sultry voice, a liaison in a glance
Craved for my attention.

Lost in a battery of desks,
Our feelings bounced off walls
To drown themselves in business patter,
Illicit meetings, inconsequential chatter,
Talk of ideology, fruitless plans for sharing,
But was it real, did we understand
The link between flirtation and disaster.

Her presence had turned me to distraction,
With the prowess of a cat
Her claws un-bared, she gently pawed
The underbelly of naivety; putty melted
And a taut gut erupted in imaginings.

We understood the rules; the barometer set fair,
But then our lot was swilled in jealous slop,
Down my cheeks ran bitter scarlet drops,
Blood filled tears which left a mist
On eyes that could not see,
The door of understanding now was locked.

It is too late now
Since the last brush of hands excited,
And a muffled snigger on the line
Shut out the tight spring of minds
Which led to the burial of two 'lovers,'
One here – the other who knows where,
Who, though parted
Were from habit stuck fast,
Knowing how to climb into each other's thoughts,
Victims, of the extra sensory.

The Box

I have it all,
Trapped in a throwaway box, it's top
Bottom and sides smooth from a touch
Which has fondled it to varnished perfection,
A touchstone to test my feelings on,
Where globe-trotting tramps have loved
And dossed in its sensual corners, and
Saintly folks have drawn their breath in gasps.

It has been my mentor, an apple store,
And on frosty nights the froth of mulled stout
Has slopped in light from a frozen lock,
Casting a shadow of pleasure on its silk walls.

This freehold obloid container, has watched
As I danced at a wedding, bowed in silent prayer,
Sheltered illicit lovers, was a crutch for my despair,
One down, without other services
An extremely desirable pad,
It is my place, a joint, a palace,
A portable, sheet-metal shack.

The Cobbled Track

I

With a little push
this walk along a cobbled track began,
whose blocks of stone were chiselled
from a clean cut fissure
in a hill of solid granite;
some which crumbled at a touch,
or when they felt
the heated longing of a simple man

II

The first few miles were easy
in winter after dark
Gran and I would walk to town,
through shadows under gas lamps,
over the bridge of a slurry river,
to a market place of stalls,
where hissing lanterns hid the shine
of antique Georgian silver; so soft
Her hands would lead me past
the queues at picture houses, near
a Theatre Royal, where usherettes
in green and brown, served coffee
with cigars to men in white silk scarves,
and women wrapped in sable stoles.
The commissionaire was big,
fat arms and legs and velvet gloves,
and down the street past ranks of cabs,
electric trams ran every hour;
outside a shop we'd smell roast pork,
and for a special treat I had
a warm meat pie, gravy dripping off my chin;

we'd stand and look at fish and crabs
laid out on sloping marble slabs;
later in a dingy upstairs room, people met
to take the laying on of hands; all healed
we'd wander back past dark stone mills.

III

Still my steps were sure, my silhouette
stood out against the backdrop sky,
razor sensitivities were honed, to protect
a dozen and a half of luckless friends.
Then to watching people pass
through market squares,
saw their worried faces
on busy thoroughfares,
beneath their icy pause
there was a warmth, and
the eyes of a doting one
was sometimes hidden there.

But are they real, do they
feel the link between,
themselves and those
they're rubbing shoulders with.

If all they have are narrow ways
which stifle, bore and then decay,
show them one who understands.
One in pain.

IV

When all there is
Is a place in the shadow
And fitful bouts of troubled rest.

When all we get
Are crumbs from a cloth of avarice
Till kinder hands are moved to share.

And stand and wait
In systems planned by fools
Until a door of understanding moves.

There is a chance
We'll have to watch a summer sky
Dissolve to winter grey.

Besides all this
We could get caught by factions.
Or revolutions from another shore.

Why should we
All compete to make the fastest riches
As a measure of success.

Without more care
This world will rot into
A planet of despair.

V

The miles got longer as I trod,
on mill, grit, flag and holy stones,
left a maze of twisted alleys far behind,
dead ends which met me face to face,
lonely on the endless straights of road.

VI

Now a walk across the holy stones,
each Sunday morning in a hall of saints;
colour purple splashed on orbs of gold.

Shafts of early sunlight pierced the dark,
to tint the vestments of a holy man,
and wash his tainted guilty shadow clean.

There to listen to the whisper of a congregation,
above me, wafting boughs on weathered slate,
saw the Cross of Life, and maybe death,
stir the half-truths in us all, when we looked
for selfish comfort from a resurrecting mind.

Ate the leavened bread, drank of holy wine,
but all that darkened eyes could see, was
the sorrow and the sadness, stored by men.

VII

Reasoning, wavering,
Satisfying, quavering
Indulge yourself you fool
Enjoy yourself in torrid tasks,
Go on, break the rule.

You'll win each one
If guile you use
And cut off all retreat,
Indulge yourself, demean yourself,
Go on, break the rule.

VIII

Then she came, lightly starched,
a popinjay in cotton printed dress,
not a lover, more a jezebel
in plum red winter fashions.

Her eyes, black iris eyes
could pin you to a cloud,
and she smelled of yellow,
newly flowered gorse.

I have watched her practice
courtship, with underbelly preened,
showing off her thighs
to tease a bevy of the boys.

Like the shiver of a brittle leaf,
the vibrato of a flute,
there was magic in her voice
which echoed down the wind.

Out of the shadow of too many sighs,
I clutched at creativity,
wrestled with virginity
on slopes of green erotic moor.

IX

Now a rest
in swirls of hops and malted air,
drinking beer
wrapped up in coils of hazy smoke,
then a walk
along a midnight wooded valley floor,
smelling
the frosted breath of stones,
and faded glass
on trellised sedge green slopes;
down the bank
of a purple brackish stream,
in the iridescence
saw the siren of the dark, a water nymph,
heard her cry
and met the gaping circles of her eyes,
as she skimmed
the surface of this inky brook,
barely human
her face I'd seen some little time before,
it was the jezebel
from that green erotic moor.

X

Epilogue

Sir,
I walked on the holes of spun webs,
all my life
felt the gossamer ladder tremble,
often caught a lucky strand
to save myself from falling.

Son,
I have watched you,
your every movement,
felt the pulse of your mind
asking for protection.
since you learned to tie
a criss-cross shoe lace,
cheated in a game of tag,
your number was booked;
I shouted it several times,
you chose to ignore it,
in fact ran in another direction.
I have tramped
across the sludge of valleys,
the pollution of peaks
to attract your attention.

Sir,
Can't you remember me saying,
look into the face of a child;
come to me;
the times I said
how mild and gentle you are,
how I tried to be a man,
a real man.
Committed myself to you
in front of witnesses,
made a pledge to love my neighbour,

sheltered the poor and homeless,
had good words
for those who hated me-
except one, perhaps two;
turned the other cheek;
Sacrificed myself ...

Son,
I know all about you,
you have done many things in my name,
others despite it,
when all your loves and hates,
rights and wrongs
come crowding back,
you and I will meet.
Face to face.

XI

The secrets of the humble and the vain,
are locked in time,
stored to harvest when dew is on the mould,
mystery imprinted on the matter of the mind,
interpreted by skilful, foolish souls.
Who put wisdom in the ground of life
for intellect to vanish, just the same?
Love is wasted among fools
where is that to heal all pain.

The Gallery

We entered the gallery hand in hand,
Unsure of ourselves on the first visit,
Our grip tightened at the severe faces,
Reminiscent of an undertaker's parlour.

Mock terrazzo floors chilled our feet
As we mingled with some who pretended to
Understand a modern sculpture, rude but proud,
And a canvas of gold with a single band of red.

We liked a painting of a ship under a bridge,
A reminder of your mother sailing to Italy,
Then a picture of "Leviathan" and "Thunderer,"
Steam train 'double-headers' thrusting thru'
War-time black-out across the Tyne Bridge,
Wheels sparkling in staccato skidding bursts.

We stood back from the landscapes, at
What we guessed was a proper distance,
A rural scene around an old cathedral,
River water lapping a shire's fetlocks,
You could almost hear the men on horseback,
Shout at frisky brown and white hounds.

And the sky, an angry daub of purple Aurora,
The green shades of darkness pressed down,
Imagined sounds of nature and a Cathedral choir,
Ushering in a twilight of early winter.
Someone said "I would like to own this."
I said "It's for the world."
The crowd dispersed.

The Rose and Crown

In this illuminated haunt
A Pickwickian host straddles the bar,
Sleeves rolled, trousers well-hoisted,
Tailored around a cosy paunch;
A starched collar bites the folds of his neck,
But with a smile on his sagging jowl
He pulls his pints of bitter with panache.
With each swing of a brass-railed door,
A cloud of smoky light and beery air
Flushes on to dark downtown pavements,
The piano rattles a ragtime song
Where hail fellows, let's have another one fellows,
Braceleted, chain slung men sit
To recall their conquest of the Costa Brava;
Stuck with the importance of real ale,
Smugly they lift their monogramed tankards
Intent on the cleavage of a bar maid.
Outside on the night streets, others prefer
To look at lamps lit on posts, straight hems
Of unseen kerbs and lonely cul-de-sacs,
Some which curve past dim suburbs,
To peter out on the edge of a moor.

The Siren of the Dark

Still and swift the siren moves o'er waters clear.
In soaring dipping circles on the brink of even-tide,
Hovers silent as the muffled pause of tears
Comes shimmering thro' the pinkish shroud of night.

Halting call of sensuous lute and lyre,
Half immersed in languid waters of the brook,
Rushing babbling liquid of the wind;
Forsaking empty shallowness of looks.

See not those prismed circles so forlorn,
Nor allow the swilling, billowing tide
To disconcert the balance, made of scorn
Of schismed beings so hungering for pride.

Currents swirling, whirlpool skirling,
Thrashing in the rage of dams strong hold;
Battling out frustrations in the whirl
Of deeds, untried, unsold.

Still hovering o'er these waters dulled with fear,
Poor sirens grasping, groping, dancing knell
Exhausted spirit tolling out its heartless jeer
Plunging step submerging down to hell.

Clearing waters of this reservoir of vain delight
Lapping out last throes of tidal swell
Designs dissolving in the quickening light
Of true, soft, liquid passions made aright.

The Sword of Damocles

Still sat beneath a hanging blade
There is no end to this charade

Which all began from that first glance
And left me in a waking trance

It was a friendship, more than special
Of warmth and trust, and blind compassion

So little choice, but be possessed
Was it just the chemistry of sex?

A man condemned, and bound to be
What's more, not wanting to be free

A mind which constantly recalls
That this was worth a life, and all

To learn to feel without a touch
And match the eyes against her looks

The blend of scent when nuzzled close
A sultry voice which stirs the most

We would sink into a velvet couch
And melt together, mouth to mouth

What was the overwhelming power?
That blossomed and began to sour

Too soon the magic ceased to be
It was now the turn of jealousy

Was it gone, the will to say 'I care?'
Perhaps I'd lost the urge to share

There must have been an aberration
But what was needed was salvation.

If only I had stopped the game,
Apologised, and took the blame

Still poised above, the sword of fears
Which brought me to a flood of tears

Forgiveness is the thing I crave
You see, I'm not conditioned to be brave.

But for all the fury, and the scorn
I'd return again, and ride the storm.

The Theatre Royal

The library is stood on hallowed ground,
Stores of unread words, diagrams and graphs
With sculptures stood on polished marble plinths,
Bizarre, fat arms and legs and leering laughs.

It's where the Theatre Royal used to stand,
With a Pit and Stalls and Circle Bar
And usherettes in bottle green and browns,
Who served the tea and coffee in the aisles.

I never went there, but I used to stare
At long frocked women, and their gentlemen,
Silhouetted in the foyer, white scarved,
Buying programmes, mints, and big cigars.

Across the road a stand for Hackney Cabs
And trams ran down the street on every hour,
But then, there was a stout Commissionaire,
Bizarre, fat arms and legs and trim moustache.

The Tragedy of Maudlin Man

Academy of stealth, pretentious,
Wherein was spun the story of a maudlin man,
Seat of learning soiled by erring minds
And lashed by Satan's thunder,
Unbalanced by insidious wiles;
In moulding vale the prologue to the end was brewed,
Disarmed on slopes of green dark moor,
Wicket fence of fate entwining heartbeats of short sanity
Encroached by spirits of undoubted view;
With faltering gait and vacant musing,
Tresses languid in the wind of hope,
Sad maudlin man, aghast, subdued, demeaning,
Held outcast in his plane of life.
So lead out poor sylph and fashion your desires,
Then shall fulfilment stir the raging, purging pyre.

Thoughts at Dawn

Now that a long night's breath
has stopped its drift across a restless bed,
I am content to dream and conjure images
cast from a magic lantern in my head.
Through drops of rain burst on window glass,
an Autumn star flees, scrambled in the wet,
slow to catch a swiftly gathered stormy cumulus,
and the smell of stones, grass flecked with dew,
pincered patterns which glint back to me,
a mirage magnified in mist on distant moors.
Smoke from the gun of a man who shot the
Sheriff in a western town, hung by a lynch mob,
now quite dead, with ash from a last cigarette
smudged across his shabby leather vest.
Is that a vineyard where today the vines
are being stripped bare, and sinewy backs
will work to load the vats to overflow,
for feet to pound the fruit to scarlet liquid,
then to drink and dance, sing the songs I know.
Or could it be a boom town of oil, pipes
cast in iron, thrust through sludge, past derricks.
No, a steel town where ice cold ingots
are stacked in rows waiting for the smelter.
Let someone else talk of cool flat rocks
in summer mountain passes, here in this room
a purple pool of light murmurs its good feeling.

Where is Haven for a Man in Quest?

I have it all, yet nothing do I have,
Though there is shelter from the elements that test
The wilt of will with need to grasp
This love called agape;
Come and bind with balm,
Pledge your love intractable,
And usher me to heights unanswerable
To places of simplicity and charm;
Sustain the germs of light and worth
In halls embellished by the good of all;
This robe of doubt was fashioned from the fruit
Of unsung passion vested in a pall;
Pointed vapour in the brain of truth
Spew out the constant itching of the call;
Who is encased in hot and cold delights?
Or sanguine passions searching for the calm;
Of regions hidden from the light of right
With senses impotent and starved;
Cry out you victims of this ruthless game
This merriment of chess to those of feeble frame;
Short lived turgid effort to connive
The sublimation of them all who came to fail;
Reluctant sponge of heated effort to survive,
Release your stifled, pented pride.

Who Will Come With Me?

Going to the ground and the peat,
Going there to the depths,
I will be there till time is spent,
Going to the ground am I;
I will release the passions of mind
'Til locked in truths survive,
You will be there in the land, say I,
Will you be there sublime?

Going to the moon and the wind,
Going there to the sky,
Why does youth anger passion?
Going to the moon am I;
I will not forsake the ken of the mind,
Nor things inbuilt to cry,
You will be there in the clouds, say I,
Will you be there refined?

THORNHILL HIGH SCHOOL
VALLEY DRIVE
THORNHILL
DEWSBURY WF12 0HE
WEST YORKSHIRE

P.M. FOSTER, M.A.

Telephone: Dewsbury 465704

PMF/PC

9th December 1987

Mr. M. Hamer,
Education Social Worker,
Oak House,
Oates Street,
DEWSBURY.

Dear Maurice,

If time permitted, I would attempt to compose a poem to express my gratitude to you. However, crisis management does not afford the opportunity for such luxuries and, more honestly, my creative talents would not adequately convey the depths of my appreciation.

I am, therefore, left with the inadequacies of my prose.

You will be sorely missed at Thornhill, for not only have you gained the respect you deserve, but you have won a place in our hearts. I'm sure you will say that you are merely a part of the furniture, but if that is so, then you are everyone's favourite armchair.

You have done an enormous amount to move and challenge the thinking of our efforts to encourage various professionals to work together in the interests of pupils and community. In addition, the accolades of parents when speaking of your support should have made your ears burn.

But above all Maurice, selfishly, I have to say thank you for what you have done for me. It is so important for a Head to have such a sensitive and wise counsellor. You have been a valued guide and mentor through many of my heart searchings.

In short, I shall miss you.

Love

Pat

Poetry competition

HERE are the final poems from the latest entry. Now that the competition is closed, we can get down to the serious business of short-listing the poems for the cash prizes.

Around 30 poems will be chosen and sent off to the distinguished poet Stanley Cook, who will then have just over a week to make his decision on first, second, third and fourth prizes. It won't be easy. There are a lot of fine poems in many different styles and on many different subjects.

That will make judging hard, but is a boon for the next stage of the project, the compiling of our Anthology of Local Poetry. We want that to be a varied and truly representative selection of the best poetry from Huddersfield. It will be a splendid collection.

The winning poems will appear in the Examiner on Friday, October 2, and poets whose work has been selected to appear in the anthology will hear from us the following week.

Meanwhile, the Examiner and the Poetry Business would like to thank everyone who took the ti̶̶̶̶ trouble to send us poems

---

They Are Building A Hill

It is perfectly clear
that that is what they are ̶
from the scaffold̶̶
and th̶̶̶
h̶̶
th̶̶

Tre̶̶
pres̶̶
They̶̶
until̶̶
Yellow̶̶
about ̶
with lo̶
cement,̶
and gras̶
Men in y̶
study wha̶

Did they g̶
for this hil̶
It could blo̶
or a public ̶
Where can o̶
Will it be rig̶
it?

Will it fit in w̶
The one next t̶
but they've bee̶
for years now, ̶
and it still isn't ̶

★
A Final ̶

Nature has its way o̶
how easy it is to lose̶
a loved one, departed̶
twenty years, like my p̶
pigs, they died within ̶
one another, no cause,̶
gave up the ghost, and,̶
true blue that I am, I bu̶
too soft, you may say, sh̶
flung them in the bin
along with the rest of your rubbish.
T L WEEDON
Golcar

★ ★ ★
Revelations

Stretch out in the stubble of corn
And let straw cling to washed denim,
With your chin cupped in caring hands
Look toward the split-level habitat
Framed under the belly of a milk cow,
It is dancing in a haze, precarious on a
   spur
With garden walls bedded in flaking
   rock,
Unsure foundations, and a trellis of
   vapour trails

Poetry winners

THE competition that kept Huddersfield writing over the summer has now been judged.

The distinguished Sheffield poet Stanley Cook had the job of choosing four poems from a shortlist of 32. Here is his decision:

Equal First Prize—Graham Bretherick, **Tees Boat Trip**; Jackie Stead, **Now She Is Old**;

Third—Maurice Hamer, **Revelations**;

Fourth—Martin Murphy, **Sharon**.

Congratulations to these four fine poets. The poems are reprinted here. We hope you agree they are worthy winners.

The First Prize-winners will share £75 and so receive the old figure of £37.50.

Third Prize is £10 and Fourth £5.

Most important, of course, is that they will head our Local Poetry Anthology to be published in December. At least another 32 poets will join them in the collection, which we are busy compiling at the moment.

The names of the poets to be included in the Anthology and the six runners-up who win free workshops at The Poetry Business will be announced in two weeks' time, Friday, October 16.

Meanwhile, we hope you enjoy ̶̶̶ prize-winning poems.

̶̶̶ fires of a̶
crimson and gold̶
the world is old̶̶
so long to spring̶̶
Will you walk ̶̶
in the magic of̶̶
the holly berr̶̶

Our boat chugs
Through cold tea Tees and sees
The down and out
of dock de-frocked and rocked wi̶
ruin.
Proud river
Auctioned off to goulish tripper
Gawping at the aftermath
Of the death of work.

GRAHAM BR̶

̶̶̶ the dross
̶ clinging to its poi̶
mould a coral ̶

M HA̶
Castl̶

★

Which ̶̶̶

bells ring across the snow
remember.
̶ELENA STAPLES
̶eechead Road

Third prize
REVELATIONS

Stretch out in the stubble of corn
And let straw cling to washed denim,
With your chin cupped in caring hands
Look toward the split-level habitat
Framed under the belly of a milk cow.
It is dancing in a haze, precarious on a
   spur
With garden walls bedded in flaking
   rock,
Unsure foundations, and a trellis of
   vapour trails
Which distort the symmetry of a
   doomed artifact.

A trimmed poodle paws after Emperor
   butterflies,
But its pomaded fists are slow
In the cloud of incinerated compost;
Above, the map of a new world
In pleasing clerical grey, silhouetted
Against blossom pink to orange,
And edged in supernatural crimsons,
Must we wait for a golden arm to reach
   down
To massage and comfort the nervous
   systems
Of the ambitious, stressed professionals
   and factions,
Cliques, parties, mercenaries and uneasy
   militia,
The powerful and powerless?
Sieve and refine, pour out the dross
And bury this land clinging to its poi-
   sons,
Plait silken ladders, mould a coral esca-
   lator,
And climb.

MAURICE HAMER

̶ in
sop-
me
ground,
ildren to
̶ or sleigh-
bloody-well
ear round.
̶LL STAPLES
̶eenhead Road

99

www.ingramcontent.com/pod-product-compliance
Lightning Source LLC
LaVergne TN
LVHW011407080426
835511LV00005B/425